Conversations with Coherent Worlds

Also By Anusha Sridharan :

Mixture is the New Secret
Picturesque Aromas of Thought Alleys

Anusha Sridharan

Conversations with Coherent Worlds

First published by Lapsus Creations in India.
An imprint of Lapsus.

ISBN - 13 : 978-81-942112-3-5

MRP – INR 250

Illustrations by Manish Kumar.
Layout by Simran Munot.

Printed and Bound in India by Thomson Press India Ltd.

Published by Lapsus Creations
E-mail: getintouch@lapsuscreations.com
www.lapsuscreations.com

ABOUT THE AUTHOR

Anusha Sridharan is a light hearted woman who dwells in poetry and in between abstract lines. For her, emotions and expressions serve as a medium of connections; Be it people or books, incidents or thoughts, experiences or reasons.

Her poems have been of greater contribution to many anthologies. To add more to her attainments, she also has self published 'Sky Album' and 'Picturesque Aromas Of Thought Alleys' with Amazon KDP.

Her love for art also reflects in photography and other forms. She believes that a writer is alive as long as there is a belief that there is art in everyone and everything.

DEDICATIONS

To the mighty divine and my well-wishers who have always been a supporting wing to my broken.

To my mom, who has been tirelessly the core of my being, a charm to my happiness and a guiding light in my dark.

To my mother-in-law who has always encouraged me for all my writing endeavours.

To my dearest husband, for being there always to support me at every step.

To all other poets out there, who find their expressions in poetry.

ACKNOWLEDGEMENT

Special note of thanks to all the support and encouragement I have gotten from all my friends and family.

To Lapsus Creations and Team, thank you so very much for being there all along the writing journey of Conversations with Coherent Worlds.

Part I

My Connections With The Inanimate

I call the emotions, the floating messages, the air around me-inanimate connections. Poetry brings out the realm of my conjuncture with them. With words and flows, my thoughts structure around them to give out an intricate reflection that's expected of us to redefine and pay attention to.

Miss The Existence

There is a lot to flow, to run by, pass by,
Like those revisits to the memory loves.
Much awaited gathering;
To the rather different togetherness.
Existence is a good old thing,
Not a secluded piece of ignorance.
Not unless needed, a something;
hat's strangled to oblivion.
Some struggles are hard to breathe with,
Some just breathe you in.
For more than what could be believed in,
There is trust that couldn't be trusted in.
Missing a chance to mend,
A carefree fence to send.
An existence is all what is asked,
Rather something missed and lost.
Precisely, a why, another to answer with,
To summon the lost call to try,
Why isn't be a question anymore,
For what's done is a miss at all!

A Bothered Nothingness

Nothing less to the nothingness,
A verge to the staggered path,
With the purpose kept to hold,
Of the existence to cure.
A bothered much is not of functional opposites;
But of the dominant silliness.
A kid in the mind and
Adult by heart; it is a parallel, unstopped.
Experienced by the jawlines that munched,
Of all the foods that once crunched.
Been through all and yet a doubt,
For what still remains silent
Is bothered nothingness.
Unforgiven of the outburst of piano tiles,
I sustain questioning the music that it plays,
Arranged pieces in its own aligned way,
Orderly and formed, I seem to believe;
Something that releases
The freedom prey to open land.
Slip away, of those words;
Unspoken when thought of.
An idea thought and not done,
such is the equivalent of non-existence.

Pepper Got Sugared

Tilted towards those of sugar less;
Sour armed with a bitter kettle.
Soup filled with pepper and spice,
Burn goes down with a tongue of fire.
Sugar is essential, said so too for salt.
Grain of salt hit while sugar goes to pamper.
Blind is not the taste, to tell
What a lie is and what isn't!
Probable spice is of the due sugar,
A faintly over done dose;
A reminder to the want of change,
Yet, a thing for pepper to get sugared.
Food to taste, taste buds to whine,
Well around the corner, I'd request you to stay.
Something burning of the choices;
Picky about the butter mist to prefer.
A supper be lost to the grill,
A stomach's ask would just be null.
Anything then, is a blessing;
Call it again that pepper got sweet.

Day Begins With You

The light of the sun,
The warmth of its rays,
I begin to relish the reason of my being,
Scaling my imagination to grow beyond,
Not just a musing but a missed reality.

The day begins with you.
The thought of us together,
For the souls we are bound to be,
A greater cause to serve.
Be it an interpretation or a connection,
There exists the bond
Of co-existence between us.

At noon, we mark our disappearances,
Questioning our powers
At the brim of sun's peak,
Blended with the white, we shall,
Like we are of the kind, that's found within.

Ends to map us both,
Like a route to find us on shore,
Of a treasure that we are,
Day and night, we form that every flip.

A Future To Make

A stare, mild settlement
Of the fights fought,
With the self, to seek answers for.
To be less infused of,
Somewhere, within loss of the source of rent,
A source to discover an outlet.
To infer, a qualification to be,
To decide if the choices made were right,
Owned for a purpose,
A reason greater than being.
Because sometimes, things aren't how they are
Meant to be, causes to conclude
Unrealistic dead-ends to sweet.
Wary of the routes, none to have met,
Lesser of the context to relate,
Of the passed times, and less to recover.
A cost to be paid,
Of the things taken for granted
Marked for the preciousness they hold,
A still to behold,
Of the values & worth they carry.
A mild settlement, you'd call,
Of the past & present,
To console of a future to make.

Question The Pity

Some asks are rather certain,
Uncertainty is a mask of unknown.
What could you predict and not ask?
To say is, all will, great and mighty things.
Pity, oh why would I?
On what? For a chance given not right?
Risen have the questions,
Not a challenge to have them answered.
Found them unworthy to seek,
But for the questions to form, not enough?
Answers are lazy daisy,
Shine bright in the day, lose sight in the night.
Mark what may, a pity?
A lost word to the skim;
A brush through and by,
Lessens down the whole time.
'Why' is not a question anymore,
It is of need to know,
A reason & a purpose,
So, you, question that pity!

Suggestive Irony

Belief is a strange ask,
Unwilling to the misty land.
Known to the existent,
A surprise to the unheard.
What could be a stranger deal,
Than an ask to the want
Given and not taken,
But be taken without given?
Shall I retain the suggestion
Once made to state a pun?
That turns facts into irony,
A bliss of the blind delusion.
I play a game to find,
To seek and know;
Things waiting ahead in time,
For a memory of past.
A place to be sunken around,
Slip away to sun & dance,
Bravery isn't a town,
Ship to the suggestive irony;
Is a blend to be in.

Mockery Done Right

Oh Why! Would you mock?
Even when the clock says tick-tock.
A sound that meant right,
Pun to the sudden sight.
Playfully light, a pause too bleak
Yet, to the needs not so weak.
Substance to the glory in offer,
Childish would be to accept and ignore.
Mind the symphony to the blanks,
A trace to the backs to begin
Another to a fine sign,
Brings a deal of great zeal.
What a craze would it be
For mockery to screech,
A crawl to bury;
Yet some another to preach.
Mockery done right;
A glee to unknown flaw,
So much to the more
I skipped to know gnaw!

Only If You Knew

Even before you think you know,
Across the told and see,
Hear the loud of the silence;
Contemplate the comprehensions of unspoken.
Similar to the sensed
Heat from the barren ground,
Sown be the reaped fruit,
Seeds again to another dawn.
Woken up for sudden charge,
Subtle a sojourn to hallway's bridge.
Gazed around to known flaw,
Arisen to release the mistaken.
Causes known for mergers;
In townships for the wars.
Clashes to the power of preach;
Yet, undone to the followed stints.
Only if you know there is,
The untimely gasp of conquer,
Fallen in, yet again the intent
And purpose of the war begins.

Starting With The Masses

Masses be the equal crowd,
Quite a while to the swarm.
Like the bees do some ground magic;
Into the wind blow with fragrance.
Indent with the loss of certainty,
Hidden are the intentions & constants.
Built upon a mask, being an ask;
There is no answer to the flow with time.
Need is bound to pile, a relation to form.
Advancing in future to split,
The time is a challenge, you'll yet face.
For, it's a keeper and you're just a watcher.
Smitten by the lake of demand,
Following a herd, losing the identity,
Alarmed is my soul, bolted in the web
Towards building the courage, to be, to die.
Lagged between the time,
Elapsed are the moments,
Flows again with the masses,
A plot of emotions to drain & train.

A Discarded Offense

A discard is not of what was needed,
Be it of those, potential to cause hurt.
A trust be guarded inside the warmth,
Cause the burn if the heat goes away.
Tendency to believe things kept in faith in,
Due be the respects if accepted wrong.
Assumptions made along the way,
Worthy or not, so shall time will say.
Any offense that be,
The remark of let down to expect
What cry shalt thou, pierces to know
The truth, so sour and ugly.
Unruly it be, for to go unnoticed,
Why some are unseen, known yet, ignored.
Ply the things implied,
Reasons unknown & marked just.
Questioning is no game,
Need to find, a risen reality.
Some answers, lost in fallacy,
Find out, some, of where they belong.

Keeping Quiet

Silence within, tackled and suppressed;
You could ask a hedge of why.
Some stakes, the mind games, one is lost;
Within the conflicts of thoughts.
Kept a secret, hidden grief,
Cried in dark, bowed in vague relief,
Unaware of the whole of times,
Quiet I was, for all said and echoed.
Orients within the sigh of preparedness,
A trust broken, as far for the things
Shouldn't have been spoken.
A regret it be, still alive;
For sharing things a little too much.
Keeping quiet, a bliss, a harmony;
A symphony to the casting emotions.
Filmed be they, like the changing times,
Lighted towards the things to come.
Just say as much apt as needed.
Not a word more or less;
Nothing more to lose, nothing less to pledge,
A contract with self, to sustain.

Reading Your Voice

Conservations read in my head
Broad and wide; fresh in my memories,
Of the happy times, been in to be in,
All in a memory to last and relive.
Observed the way you spoke,
Each word had something to mean,
Ignorance, you may call it.
For, all I have you were heard,
Just a melody to my ears.
Happiness, be a state, as portrayed,
I shall then dream to make that dream.
Reading voices, a tell of interpretations
Masked and baked, to a new cookie cake,
To consume, and along the way, to digest.
Remembered all the arguments.
So, as you said things that we fail at;
To understand each other;
For whatever we had to say.
No longer was the sync.
Words blurred, meanings contain
What's said, what's meant;
Things stayed known and bent.

A Ladder's Permit

Everyone stops at the summit,
Set the limits to the sky?
Who gives the authority of limits,
When the lines are not set by us?
The limits of achievements aren't stationary,
They are more ahead in time, with time.
That's how the progress is meant to be,
To give ladder's permit, its full potential.
Fly along the clouds from the sky,
They are just like co-passengers
Waiting to travel with you,
For them, you are their visionary.
Birds flow like the mind's whisper
Yet, so high and high,
The heights are no reachable,
If assumed & limited to set bar.
Rise above the standards,
Get better than the best.
No one set a ladder's permit
Unless, you called it on yourself.

The Unkempt Hole

Gambit is just a play;
Mimicry as dawned to the plight in slay.
A pieced reminiscence is doubtful cue,
Another hole to gain distasteful clearance.
Changes to charge
Decrees to consider and to coerce with.
Possibilities are panache, loud and vibrant;
A persistent miracle waiting to happen.
Call it a subtle changing, towards the unkempt
hole,
Precursor to build, caging the armour's gauge,
Set again to play a sublime role.
Unimagined thoughts or so, a chilled grain;
In the connected soul,
Marking the presence, untold, unsettled,
An imagery to showcase.
Bring on the adjustment to dodge,
A case to make a plea; a realization,
Of the certainty in the unkempt.

What's the Difference In Being?

Difference in being submerged;
Volatility is in the state of existence.
A plight filled with pity;
A regret that is watchful.
Cared enough, did we? To mend things;
That should have been, not that the way it is;
Of the things it could have been.
No takers for non-believers,
So is the case for those beliefs;
But, done nothing so that it works.
What's the difference in being?
A question that arises; a pulse brings in.
Questioning the very cause of being alive,
Else; what's the use with unresolved & un-
worked.
Worth of life, measurable, not so easy;
Quantifiable or tangible is a memoir
Of obstruction & abstraction.
A consistent belonging of reliance,
A pause to self-reflection.
A declaration to retrograde
To the beginning from the new ends.

Stolen Charge

Before all the wandering started;
Shall I take a moment to charge?
Of all the things I am to pass on;
Do I carry some along with me?
Primarily, if I were to walk the talk;
I shall be the merit to stack.
But for things to come and go;
The generations are bound to see & follow.
A stolen charge, is what I'd call a lost permit;
To something unique & undefined.
Of the set limits & heights;
Only some are shown a way to.
Unknown paths are less talketh of,
Of the uncertainties, the fear to bring.
A relation, it is for the searches to result;
May of the queries, of the lost and traded.
Charges of stolen nature, is a cry of calls.
What time could change, if a stolen is returned?
A charge could be a deal changer,
For all the regards of the returned & possessed
values.

Collecting What You Lost

What to do for the things lost,
How would one regain what's lost?
To reclaim what we had once owned,
How to reestablished of one's possessions?
Of the lost possessions, would the value remain the same?
Or would the worth increase multifold?
A trail of never-ending thought shall form,
To reconnect & kindle the lost worth.
Collecting what you have already lost?
Is that an easy job? Oh, no!
For sure, it is not.
It takes a tremble down,
A grief filled cry from the lost hopes.
What's left if you ask,
I'd say, "the hope of becoming worthy, yet again."
To make all those sacrifices
Not go in vain, but in favour of a greater cause.
What's lost can't be forgotten,
But what's lost can be shown to be; worthier.
A realization is asked for,
to fulfill the last wish of the lost.

The Kept Distance

As a dialogue it might seem,
Changes that keep happening, as to suggest,
slightest,
While across the seas of inertia,
Season of need to change persists.
The distance kept, for sighed,
Less be the agony, to rise, to give;
A suggestive blend of precarious plunge
Taken and granted, a fisted cage.
Aversions to the crazes built
Distances but seem as the vision.
Careful yet, might seem bothersome,
Some uncontrolled & unguided lies.
Believe it to be true, off to be false,
A safe distance from reality,
Care-free of the disruptive illusions;
Those of the imagination & cries.
Stab to bear, spear to spare.
How far could prayer lead,
A hope that survives, yet another dream.
The kept distance, farther away to limit.

Did You Dream Today?

"Did you dream today?"
a question asked among the crowd,
The more said, "yes", the less said,
"We can afford to…".
Surprised answers come around the floor,
The stranger it got, with the cheers & cries
Floating as the aura of the room.
Some dared to dream with their wings cut.
Some scared to dream,
To let live with the rest that they have got!
"What is scary?" and "why is it a dare?",
Two questions racing in my head,
Why is anyone's fault to dream?
Crazier than it sounds,
The fear it is, within, of failures.
The fear of not being able to raise again.
Why is it such a chance?
Why could it not be a model,
To rise up stronger the very time we fall?
The weaker you are towards your goal,
The lesser you dream about it.

The stronger you are, the lesser you are feared by it.
Alas! A fear to answer,
"Did you dream today?" is gone.

A Woken-Up Sleep

A sleep's portrayal, as woman of a kind,
She's dealt with all the love & care.
Everyone's precious, that she be,
For woken up sleep, it's such a bad day.
A tone of relaxation and a sense of relief,
A wild communication to the body to rest.
A subtle note of soothing settlement,
To the null and complete silence.
Woken up from sleep is a tale from other day,
A dream is a mild affection of from withins of head.
Acceptance of the dreams as part of realities,
Paves way to the grown mundane of dreams.
Be dauntless to the mock of mildness,
There's a past to be dealt with
A kind mark of nostalgia,
A gentle mindful envoy to unleash the potentials,
Of the subconscious guiding you through,
Helping in making decisions
Bold and beautiful,
Of the thoughts that are not yet heard of!

The Jammed Doors

Thrown away to agony,
To the plausible clauses of constrained desires.
Deeply pained by the controllable,
Of the uncertainties that were to be suffered.
Doors of the answers seem to be all jammed,
Some way, that can be taken,
Is waited upon, to be found.
A way out towards the end,
As though end of another hole,
A burrow once stuck inside,
A miracle to lead on to,
On the other side of dawn,
To bring new beginnings,
Let go of the posteriors past,
Meaning the material joys to realize by.
Bay to circumvent,
A layer to enrich, uncover;
Of the jammed doors,
For the hidden realities are not to be found.
But be faced and succumbed by,
For the doors are jammed,
But not for the screaming desires!

False Pretense

A breakthrough of serious asks,
A false pretense of concern,
Not none, not bothered,
To care to suggest a solution.
Not that there's route form
Always thought as welcome,
But the windows & doors were left closed,
For wants to avoid the intrusions.
It is all a lie,
For the protection of the glass like view,
To be in an illusion,
Settling with no wonder of strands.
Smiling away with glory,
As it fades off my face,
A pretense as though it would occur,
Harder than it should seem
To compress & compromise,
A tag, a far beyond approach,
To cease, to refrain from the idea of existence.
Specifics of the course of action,
Mending the ways through & above,
Boundaries to pass,
Rules to break, Illusions to deny!

Miss Mistaken

Miss mistaken as they would call me,
For the arguments that I created for myself,
The tiny fragile sentiments that I hit,
Knowingly or unknowingly,
A trail that I leave,
For someone to mock my feelings,
Hurting & assembling my broken pieces.
Fragments as I gathered,
Bits and pieces, of myself as I align,
Mistaken to be a coward,
But the boiling blood inside me,
Is still on the rise.
For all the times that I have been mistaken,
For something I am not,
For someone I am not,
And for all the things made me responsible,
And result of me,
That were never started as the source of me!

Skilled Connection

Skills of the mortal minds,
Wavering like the function of minds.
Isn't that a connection to have,
To unwind the loops of missed possessions?
What to be done with skills had,
To help, to survive and die one day.
A cycle in itself from birth to death,
Still bygone with an element of mystery.
Synergy, the willingness to grow & teach,
Connection of the skill from one to another,
From the master of art to the mastery,
A long way to go,
Yet, a most sustained way to progress.
Connections too deep, enthusiasm to seek,
A link to form, a bridge to build,
With the similar mind to join forces,
A need of cause & to squad in place.
Profoundness to flaunt, execution to commit,
A planned state of future that's decided.
Come to form, of the beginning to make,
A connection to discover, a comrade to take.

Talk to Me

A voice from within calls out,
A cry too loud, to head & act.
Loudness to comprehend, intensity to demystify,
A concern to raise and voice out.
To vent, to liberate, to free thyself,
Of all the qualms & grief,
To let in the vibes of positivity to flow in,
To end the darkness wild & dense.
A little too fond, of the uncertainty,
The load of puzzle to carry all along,
To discover remnant ways to invade,
To resolve the unknowns & mark the certain.
Try too hard, not so for some use,
Cause the puzzles too change with time,
Flowing away taking a form that's different,
Leading to yet a new journey to conclude.
A realization that devices inside you,
On your way towards the method of solving,
A voice within, knows it all,
And that has experienced it all.

Endless Pause, Forever?

As much I want the time to cease,
I realize the control isn't with me.
To possess the power to mend and blend,
I shall have to wait
To dream again,
Where I do have controls
Of what I see and continue to dream about.
Some are pleasing,
The others are just those nightmares
That I want to escape.
Of the two kinds,
I derive not the lessons,
But experiences of my thoughts,
Venting out their suggestions to me.
A pause to reflect is what I ask for.
With busy times and passing deltas,
I got less time left with me.
A forever, motionless speed,
The driving force,
With no displacement,
Flamboyant by nature,
Of which I figure an endless pause.

Prayer's Prominence

A strong belief, a radiance,
Of the faith that you carry in your heart,
The power that it retains you with,
Is prominent.
Gives you the feeling,
A confidence to be hopeful again,
A stronger will to succeed,
And to be devoid of all the worries
That could bog you down.
Don't deprive yourself
Of the power that you can attain,
With a simple prayer's prominence,
Of the well-being,
And for the greater good of the common.
Those summonses of reassurances,
Of the restored state of peace,
Limit not the boundless,
Faith be that magic,
To keep along and hold on to.

The Guilty Stood Aside

Of the crimes,
Committed and intended of,
Is the regret still within?
Or is it the end so loosely looped,
That there isn't any desire;
To mend things rightfully?
A chance,
Given if, to make things alright, and do it better,
Would one still take a chance to cut the cord?
Where the guilty stood aside,
And there is the culprit
Who let it happen,
So free & careless; on the roam.
A standing of the choice,
Of the side you stand by,
The good or evil.
But aren't they both,
Within one?
Is that choice crystal or Just that you chose to
step aside?

A Lost Root Logic

All my locus points,
Lost their way.
I didn't know how far I was from the roots.
And then there were zeroes,
Which I fail to understand.
Carries no value,
Yet has the potential to take it all,
At a snap, in one go!
Root logic wasn't a proposition,
It was rather a sign of symmetry,
To meet the nil,
To be empty.
To train to drain,
Into nothing,
A graph to build,
A route to follow,
A stability to find,
With my margins,
And the root-locus.

Masked Weapon

A race that brews inside,
Making yourself a weapon to be,
To protect,
All those dreams;
That you desire to fulfill.
It hasn't been easy,
For anyone, from the bygone pasts,
To differ from the mask you see.
Of the some you wear,
Of the some so camouflaged,
Of those that take a hit on you,
Of those you deny.
All those are masked weapons,
Some that protect you,
Some that deceive you,
Some other that lock you within the false realities.
Navigate with yourself,
For you be the strongest,
To decide,
What to stay with,
And what to abide by.

Remotely Impulsive

As opposed to nature,
Of the very being,
To step against,
And prove your point,
To put across your views; your way,
Slightly deliberate,
Rather impulsive; at times,
To not ignore,
The discriminations and the bias.
Remotely agitated
By the unreasoned mess,
A purpose to call, the culprit of misinterpretations,
To understand, in a way,
That's favourable to you.
Analogies to battle,
To make sense that's nearer to reality,
And not perceptions.
To see through the prisms,
Of the scattered obliterations,
To conjure, confess and possess,
A realization to self,
To collide in a fair conclusion.

Skeptical Mist

Scoffing and quizzing,
A job filled with passion
Yet, so filled with mist,
That I can't seem to figure the undone.
I either did imagine or just lost my way,
But I sure did make a mess out of it.
Had I known the place I used to go to,
Or the one I want to go to,
I wouldn't be going somewhere hunting,
Of that one reason which made me explore;
The difficulties of perplexities.
Like a mist, faint and slow,
It gathered like a blanket around me,
Making me surrounded with lucid thoughts,
Which trapped me in the eerie garden of bliss.
So were the roads, flattened by my thoughts,
Heavy weighted and so crushed,
With the withered grains of strayed escapes
Into the peaceful abode of disguised air.

Wrestle, It's Important

Whistle out worries,
Cook all your dilemmas,
Figure out what you need to eat,
Chew only what you can take in,
I might not know what's right, as of yet!
But, I know, for sure, I'll figure it out along the way.
As much I have refrained from writing,
I have grown to boil myself out,
To someone who defies to be self-sufficient.

Wrestle with self, it is important,
Fight your thoughts,
To see and understand,
Beyond what you already know of,
To integrate the substances of gathering,
Of both lessons and experiences,
To win yourself, a better you.

Encounters To Discover

I begin to collide with the chaos in me,
To bow in for the fears I resolve,
Yet a persistent glow that remains,
To remind me of my inability to cure.

What sustains me, questions me,
Of my value of being,
As existent I might be,
I still be quizzed of how real I am.

Perhaps, a fine sense of pride,
Over nothingness post fulfillment,
Of some desires met, resolutions set,
Re-ride, I shall to the world through unknowns.

I begin to extend, fall apart from my usual.
Join forces, I will, if needed,
To conquer my vulnerabilities,
To taste waters of my distracting illusions.

Cold breath breezes in,
Giving me a quick feel to solace,
A rather temporary version it be.
For, I have encounters still to discover.

Talking Stick

A humble man said, "Listen to all",
A wise man then added, "But do what you will".
A series of understandings then began,
To understand the two.
A stick as it assumes, shape and voice,
To will, and let the world listen,
To pass on a message "subtle",
To let thrive for evolution to lighten.
A bargain to call,
To buy or sell, as though a deal,
To collide and conclude,
To reach a common ground.
A collaborative effort, seemingly
To intend and describe, the implications, to the master,
Of the choices made, distilled on,
To a clearer state, of prior; to the latter.
Latency it be, to process on,
Perhaps the miscommunications,
Like those of the delayed attempts,
To magnify and simplify, to stand a note,
To settle on one, a neutral state.

Part II

Themed Aspirations

Special thanks to my friends, family and aquaintances for contributing their ideas to my collection. I have used the themes given by them as a base to build on these pearls. For me, the source of inspiration begins from wherever I see a start and it can begin anywhere, with you, right now, right away.

1. Word: Equinox, Color: Red, Given by: Navdeep

2. Words: Girl baby, Bravery, Society, Climate change , Millennium gals, Color: Blue, Color: Grey, Theme: Future humans and their lives, Given by Preethi Suresh.

3. Theme: City life & its surrealistic nature, Given by Koushik

4. Theme: About love from blind person's perspective, Given by Vikash Kumar

5. Word: Blood, Color: Purple, Given by Anirban

6. Theme: Gothic fantasy, "Love" story of a human and a centuries old vampire, Color: Colorful vs. Dark fantasy: Amber, Bright Green, Electric Violet, Given by - Keerthana Venkatesh.

7. Word: Curious fascination, Color: Blue, Given by Sundeep Agarwal.

8. Word: Cacophony, Color: Lavender, Given by Akanksha Singh

9. Theme: "A giant who never made anyone feel small", Given by Aniket Jain

10. Theme: "Failure will pass away, do not let the success defeat you" and "In a mad world, only the mad are sane".
Given by Vipul Singh

11. Themes: "Society is like a politician; it never lets us live or die in peace" and "Self-respect and Caste are like Oil and
Ghee/Water". Given by Dharun Aditya Senthilkumar.

12. Themes: "Are we to be like vehicle rider in our life, just seeing in front of us, navigating with the moving companions, giving attention to signals, carefully driving etc. Is there not a similarity/analogy?" and "People look very happy, are they really so? Don't they have sorrow buried in their hearts? Vice Versa – people.

13. look very unhappy, do they not have happiness at all?" and "Swan can tell water from milk". Given by a close family member who wanted to stay Anonymous.

14. Theme: "Escapism" - The tendency of a person to seek pleasure/entertainment/relief by choosing to temporarily put his otherwise mundane life on hold and seek
otherwise mundane life on hold and seek a fantasy of his own." Given by Siddharth Arunachalam.

15. Theme: "Every existing thing is born without reason, prolongs itself out of weakness, and dies by chance." Given by Chandrasekar Venkatesh.

16. Themes: "If negative emotions are stronger than positive ones. A double negative trump negative one."
"Always be afraid, to be afraid."
"There is no meaning in life, only sense."
"Precision and patience are rambunctious weapons of excellence."
"Logic tried to move an argumentative wall with a thousand reasons, a smile passed by and blew the wall down."
Given by Dakshin.

17. Theme: "Art of passing the journey called Life". Given by Divyang Hemnani.

18. Theme: "Everything comes at a price, good, bad, ugly, everything…" Given by Rishik Sharma.

19. Word: "Ambition", Color: Red. Given by Saurabh Garg

20. Words: "Hope", "Perseverance", "Breathe", "White Noise". Given by Harshini Kadari.

21. Theme: "Being You". Given by Sharannia Pillai.

22. Theme: "The things you romanticised slowly turning less desirable".
Given by Nisarga R

23. Word: "Diversity". Given by Karthik Dhawan.

Death By Chance

"The longer the weakness prolongs,
The more I get to live",
Says someone who describes death;
This in particular, a death by chance.
There is a loop the life caters to,
Of the cycles pre-destined,
Yet some agree to disagree,
That there's no decided purpose,
Of the very existence.
It is but merely an inadvertent formation,
As though probabilities of existences,
Are distributed among the chances.
It is a map that keeps changing,
Along with the changing stories,
And destinations, sliding with muted destinies,
In perimeters of the connected parallel universes.
Death in one, is just by chance,
But in the other,
It is all multiplexed arrays of oozing futures.
A declaration to remind,

Of Vernal, Summer, Autumn and Winter,
As they come and return,
In a persistent manner of their own,
Equinoxes and solstices.
Looking up to phenomena as these,
Experiences last like recurrent learnings,
A visual to record,
Mark its beauty
To adore, and realize,
The uniqueness binds us all.

Brave

Starting with a life,
Told always you were weak,
Born a girl, a fault of mine?
Stand by, no one did,
But me, my brave and my will,
To prove the world
Of all the wrongs,
Judgements formed without my consent.
Stop not,
Did I, there,
To put an end,
To all the doubts and questions,
Of my capabilities and worth.
A worth full,
For centuries to last,
A women,
To pass on the baton,
For more generations to come,
Always a race,
Always there's judgement,
But I fear not,
I stay to lead.

Life 2090

Around the corner,
Super-fast, like a bullet train,
Sped up to the future,
Of stakes of alien like humans,
Less of humanity,
More of machines,
Less of compassion,
More of algorithms.
Rewarding it rather be,
Developing tech and undue comforts,
A cause of scarcity,
Long list of deprivations
For mankind,
Of the regulars and basics,
Amenities be lost,
Be fought for.
A future,
Without a vision,
We all be doomed;
A chance, still around, to return,
Make the difference,
When we still can!

City Suburb Stand

Surreal, so dreamlike,
Cemented to be held,
Like a gathering piece of art.
From the starts of mundane,
To mechanics of machine,
Monotonous and real-like
Yet, a programmed life.
Agendas set for the days,
Part of a cycle,
Days in and out,
A pattern in this beauty,
A regular, a routine to stick on to.
With a mix of extremes,
A little bizarre,
Of the intercepts and notions,
Coarse or so, a course in its own way.
Lessons, voiced and called out,
To repair and reprimand,
To sustain the present better,
To provide a finer future,
To the many more generations to come.

Blind Love

Who calls it love, the one who can't see?
The flaws, as they aren't, to the eyes who see.

Why is the question so important?
For it isn't truly unconditional,
A matter of fact, where the love alone succeeds.

I don't see, I breathe,
The enigma, of my riddled world,
The beauty of the love, as I wonder,
Of how it would be, if I am able to see.

Isn't the love that is blind,
For the blind, a line of sight?
Perspective, rather a gain,
For a blind, to not see, but see with heart,
A plain yet, colourful theme.

Unlike, the rather routine,
Of love conveyed in ballads and poetry,
Materials things, physical possessions,
Mine stays blind and unconditional,
Expressed only in the way I see.

Purple Blood

The time I fainted,
I knew it was my last
breath as I took, the one of the pasts,
Devoid of any more oxygen that I could take in.
I floated off my frame
Up in the air,
Like some angelic possession I was to make,
An out of body experience as you might call.
Soothing and relaxing,
As I see it now,
Unbiased and varied,
Of countless streams,
Multiples of my cells
Re-engaging my army,
To flow in, as part of the system.
The marrow down awaits us,
The purple fountain I am led into,
Now is the time to rise again,
A new blood generation.

Gothic Gunther

Beauty of the paranormal,
Special than the severed normal,
I met the love of my seasoned life,
At the death of her last breath.
A life that I once lived,
Changed once for all,
After the life she transferred onto me,
A blessing from her vampire world.
Gunther they all call me,
But I call her my hunter,
As she hunted for my blood,
That old night,
A thousand years ago.
Our worlds diverted for good,
For us to converge in love,
For the unison we were about to make,
In this world of warmth,
A new example to set.

Curious Fascination

In admiration,
Of my curious interests,
I still look out for the reasons,
To ponder and discover.
Fascination, yet another channel
Serves like a captivating power,
Pulling me towards the path of exploration.
Like a soul,
Bitten by a snooping bug,
I sulk in the light of mystery
Until, the finding has been made.
There is so much more to explore,
And so less time to waste,
To the wind the thoughts to mill,
To create way for new air to renew.
Star lands and earthly spaces,
Several spectacles to conquer,
Build inferences more than possible fantasies,
There is no single final destination,
There are countless such.

Cacophony

Thunders and blenders,
Make the same kind of noise,
As though a rhythm they try to compose,
Something to show and send out loud,
A message, that they have arrived.
A culmination of several notes,
Seeming to the mix of beats,
A musical journey,
Sounding together,
A chaos of a kind,
A breathing, occurrence of dispersion,
A pattern to form,
Collisions to connect,
Crests to cross,
A distinctive music to unite.
Baritones to the nightingale's lullaby,
A cuddling warmth,
Whole in all,
One within the other,
A playful tone all across.
Uproarious and loud,

As a mark of power,
A make of dominance,
A cacophony,
A disagreement to sounds,
Yet sung together,
To find harmony is these disharmonies.

Gentle Giant

Magnificent by size and height,
May one call you a giant?
But you show no bias,
To any small, big or equal as you.

A gentle and kind,
Not a creature but epitome of empathy,
How are you this wonderful;
All big and mighty?

Treat you do, both the parts, good & bad,
Like a neutral edge to all.
Never have you been any dominant,
To the ones who you could thrust your power on,
Regarded all of the kind you best could,
Such an example of humbleness you are!

By our hearts and nature's gesture,
Together too can't make one; as big as yours,
What an honour it be,
To teach the kids of the next,
About you and the kind you are.

Fostering within us,
A sense of duty,
And compassion amongst all,
A symbol you be,
An ideal as known.

Humility – Seed: Success

All the kinds,
Of the successes and failures,
Neither to set a trend,
Of what you are,
Or you are capable of,
But just a measuring scale.
Let it not affect your head,
Strain your heart,
If you don't pass a goal,
There are chances,
Many so…always ahead.
Should you also not,
Be filled with pride,
Of things you have achieved,
And not take things for granted.

Pinch Of Madness

In a mad mad world,
We are all so mad.
Amongst us,
Aren't we sane of the all?
A tank of wise,
As though together,
As different parts of the same device.
Mad is not definition,
It is a feeling,
Of an expressed emotion,
In the long-lasting singularities.
A recipe to make the mad,
Is the pinch of all,
In this sane sane world,
We are all so mad.

Society, A Politician

Doesn't let you win or lose,
Leaves you in a fix,
Wondering what exactly you did,
That went so so wrong.
Although thought as a governing,
It is just nothing but a bothering,
Un-required, but disguised as essential.
As they define,
Becomes a law,
That is for you to abide,
But not in regard,
Of what you intend,
Or your reasons for your actions.
Such a politician, a chosen like ruler,
Although the difference being,
You don't really have a choice.
The society you be in,
Isn't by the company you keep,
It is wherever you are,
You are anyways still on the radar.

Immiscibility Of Caste & Respect

What if the discrimination was never to stop,
Hindering your purpose of the very need of one?
Respect and Caste,
Aren't of the same miscible kinds.
Although ductile,
Both are,
In their very own way,
Stretch longer than required,
Mixing up with one another,
And yet still won't be a part,
Of the other.
One talks about what your make is,
And the other tells where you get to be made.
While you need both to be what you are,
They are both a sincere mess together.
Not for comparison,
But for the show of dominance,
Of what's to hold the order,
That is higher than the rest.

White And Black Lies

Any lie told,
Has a reason of its own,
Than of a little less known,
That they exist of both kinds,
Of one of black and the other of white.
A favour for one,
A drawback for the other,
A save for some,
A punishment for the others.
What a lie or a truth be,
For the perspectives are biased,
Drawbacks in way,
Ascertain in another,
As though parallel perceptions congregate.
All lies aren't alike,
Unlike the source of how they are perceived,
A confinement of truth,
As they are in a way are.
Whites & Blacks,
Are hand in hand,
All play and good in, and the other.

Swan Philosophy

Call the milk and water apart,
By knowing just its virtue,
An art, it truly is.
It is a philosophy,
Of the identification,
Not by how one perceives,
But by rather how one is able to distinguish.
Like a lotus,
Knows the difference,
By the weight of the dew drop on it,
Accepts it as a part,
But never becomes one with it.
Open your wings to all possibilities,
Leave no excuse to not have had a chance,
There is always a way,
Waiting to be taken by you,
For you are destined,
To be walking to your next stop.

Escapism

In our mundane lives,
We are always on the lookout for escapes.
Unfaithful to our asks,
We deny changes, rather ignore,
And yet complain about the routine lives,
That we lead on.
If this isn't called escapism,
Then that else is?
But then, there are dips of fantasy,
That take you away from reality,
For a while,
Giving you a sense of satisfaction,
Of welcoming yourself to the new world,
Where all what you wish for, aligns at once.
There's sure another possibility,
Of have been bored out of desires,
For they are too evident and existent,
That you fear you'll lose your traces.
You need to stick to such dreams,
That doesn't let you sleep through the night,
For you are still at the verge of opening to achieve it.

Equinox

Equal hours apart
Within the longest and shortest,
Steams like right at the start,
Occurs in time, with multiples of two, a pair,
And a four, in a year,
To bring and make all seasons count.

Like the night to be, and the day to come,
Were to be as equal as they should be.
Time doesn't cost,
But the rotation does
With a tilt to make a mark,
Of its own,
To rule it, like it's never been said before.

Afraid To Be Afraid

Fears steal the show,
Take the light of your light,
Keeping you in the dark of your dark.
Afraid if you are,
Then be afraid that you are,
For you wouldn't want to try,
Beyond your fears.
Let not the fears put a full stop,
To your desires and dreams,
That you have always been fond of,
Only so, for you fear,
So fear to be afraid,
And afraid to be afraid,
For that it stops you;
From being what you could be;
If not for the fears you are trapped in.
Grow above and beyond,
For fears are powerless,
If you believe in yourself,
That you are capable of,
Whatever you are stubborn to accomplish.

Precision And Patience

All the marvels ever made,
Are so flawless,
Not just by experience,
But also by precision
And patience in a combination.
It is do with your will to make something perfect,
Along with the effort you agree to put in,
For all that is required for you,
To be part of that perfectness,
That you have taken up to build.
They are all parts of this big jigsaw,
The more you solve them,
They more you know about the pieces,
About where they fit,
And how to make them fit,
At times,
Because not always is something,
An else's fit.

Logically Un-Reasoned

It isn't logic, it is sense.
Everything might have a reason,
As much as it doesn't,
But it is always to do with sense,
Of what it is made of.
Logics and reasons,
Don't go all well together,
And yet they both arrange a base
For each other.
What still holds valid,
Is by sense,
And not reason
By heart,
And not what's rational,
Unless the sync forms;
Between the heart and mind,
Logic and reason,
Are all same,
Part of the same family,
Driven by a purpose,
For a cause that is dear to heart,
And the mind agrees.

Journey Called Life

Terrains of all kinds,
Wonderful at its best,
A mixture,
To experience,
To learn,
And to impart,
All the steps as part of the journey,
Which we all know as life.

Everything's a celebration,
A gift of life,
A present of moments,
A culmination of past,
With the anticipation of future.

A belief to rise above,
A hope to flourish,
A desire to break open,
From the chains of illusions.

Paths intersect,
Different choices made,
Similarity stitched on, weaved into all one,
Guideways to the proximate.

Price Tag

Ultimate as they start,
An aim in life,
Of one and all,
Like a peak to achieve,
Once in a lifetime.

Everything comes at a price,
You win some,
You lose some,
Both ways you have gained,
An experience to carry,
As a pride,
To pass on,
From your bones,
To the generations to come.

A value as it holds,
there's to treasure the worth,
in the moments of realizations,
each of their meanings,
which they are destined to possess.

Ambition

Long live the eyes,
Which see the precious pearls
In the nights,
Dreaming away to the world,
Most sought and fond.
A passion that shapes you,
Makes you,
Makes you what you are,
The reason for your being,
Serving to be the base,
Of your ambition in life,
A drive within,
As though never ending;
A race to be a part of,
Always as the first,
Long as life,
Till the end of its own,
A remarkable journey,
To find the same you,
When you started,
While you end,
To where you go, resonant of the same excitement all along.

White Noise

A spur of emotion,
Like a light from within,
Feeding you with the timely calls,
An awakening, expected of you,
As you follow on with the desires,
And many of the dreams
That you need to find ways to.
The white noise,
Is a scattering of your thoughts,
Fears and more so of your weaknesses,
Waiting to test you out,
And yet proving your determination,
Towards something
That you are constantly aiming for.
Noises, aren't distractions,
They are very much the disguised trials,
Coming your way,
To knock you down,
Make you stronger,
To prove yourself, of the worthier,
More to what you decided to win,
As a prime – a factor of your targets.

Hope Within Perseverance

Diffused state of mind,
From a sense of clarity,
And a tinge of mist,
There lies a blinking confusion.
Hope that is still there,
Somewhere in the hideout,
Waiting to be found,
Gritting the way through,
To the right time that's to come.
It is all in the power of will,
A strong determination,
To succeed, through any hurdle,
That may come, tearing on,
Letting the shivers down your spine.
Sailing through, along the winds,
As they come, and come what may,
Passing on like a warrior through,
Batons to conquer;
And milestones to meet.

Worn Out

An awe, it is how it starts,
In praises and songs in glory,
Of all the lit eyes,
To achieve something,
So close and yet so far,
Like dreams,
More of the impossible kind,
Until it be reached.

Once fond so dearly of,
Slowing ageing to grow,
As less desirable,
To the time before,
You even chose to desire it.

Why is the time so dominant?
To change the choices and desires.
Is this do to with familiarity,
or the path that seems already so worn out?

Being You

Hardest of all times,
A part of you being judged for eternity,
For done both good and bad,
As though a hangman on the stand.

The toughest it be,
to be yourself,
Yet not so hard,
if you trust yourself.

All toughs and hard come along the way,
Hurdles and setbacks as you recall,
A lesson rather, like a stepping stone,
Towards success, a better you awaits you!

Change will the time,
Urging you to be a different self,
Choose to stick by your side,
And never it let aside to dark.

Testing and triggering times that resurface,
As thorns and pressing concerns,

Judging you for your intolerant self,
But, sustain and endure through,
Be a heroic message to yourself,
And there you shall see your light, shining bright!

Diversity

Unison, a beauty,
Diverse and magnified,
Of the thoughts and vision apprehended together,
A hand held civic to guide.

In a state of faith,
A forward,
No less than the burning lamp of justice,
As served straight and right,
With no twists or turns,
And no blinds to what reality is.

A power, as it builds the core,
Of the very being,
Of a life to consume within,
The diversity,
For what we are,
All kids of this mother nature.

Diverse and evolved,
Miscellaneous and manifold,
Self-proclaimed duty to serve,

For the welfare of common good.
One ought to oblige,
The gifts of togetherness,
From the nature and the whole ecosystem,
Of gratitude and giving back.

Realistic Concern

Are we all what we are
Or rather we pretend to be?
Are we happy as we show,
Or rather how sad are we,
That we are not able to?
Looking around,
Aren't we all wearing a mask?
We are something,
We seem like something else,
We want to convey something,
But we end up saying something else.
It is all part of the same traffic,
And we are all the passengers here.
We stand by the signals,
Follow it, as it comes,
With either as a favourable choice,
Or as an undesired rule.
A signal is to give you direction,
To give you the leads on your next leap,
Wait, pause and go.
They are all around you,
The ones we recognize as realistic concerns.

Part III

My Abstractions

Reflections. Affections. Transitions - These are the words rather, experiences I find myself mostly with, either because I create my abstract world with them or reiterate my thoughts with every pause of time. Although that in itself is an abstraction.

Fall For Traps

Blink of coordination, with lack of synchronism,
A deliberate lag to cause,
A system to mind,
And guide the feedback back into the system.
It is all fall for traps,
The measures of errors and interpretations,
Sly beats of candid rhythms,
All fall in place, when all undone.

Reminders all over,
To exercise a conscious right,
Of the intellect, the only sane gift,
To adhere to faith; of concrete dogma,
From the very existence to the reason of the very living.

Trap is a precept,
A notion, an imaginary binding,
To test you against your will.
You pass or not,
Is all about how to mind it,
And approach to come out of it.

Ahead Of Times

Whilst the motions are against
The tide and parcel of inertia,
Continue to be just ahead;
Of the times where momentum has taken a
pause.
Regardless of the wavelength,
Of the timelines where incidents are to align,
I try to stitch between the voids,
Where I see a thin thread connecting them both.
Like a clothing weaved into one,
The universe conspires to get all the elements
along.
At a turn, they begin to be,
A new parallel universe altogether.
Ahead of times,
Before the frills and wrinkles passed the test,
Of the sheathed model of absence,
A new fate grew into the present.
Change is season, of springs and winters,
A cyclic loop of existence,
Yet again, ahead in time,
Time sets the range.

Foolish Bait

Like a fool, I took the bait,
Not that I get a chance all the time.
Chances are masked setbacks
Only to test you to take it.

While I chose the right,
Choices made me feel the opposite.
A bait, seemingly favourable,
Not so, only to be realized later.

Not everything leads you the same way,
To the same destination.
Paths taken are different,
Needful so, to be aware of the chosen.

Not by the outcomes, but by the journey,
Measure your success,
For you learn a lot more, through than end,
While you reach where you intend to.

A fool only sees the output,
A wise also sees the input through the output,
Like a feedback, to re-run to mend ways,
To achieve something the way they must.

Ahead Of Times

Whilst the motions are against
The tide and parcel of inertia,
Continue to be just ahead;
Of the times where momentum has taken a pause.
Regardless of the wavelength,
Of the timelines where incidents are to align,
I try to stitch between the voids,
Where I see a thin thread connecting them both.
Like a clothing weaved into one,
The universe conspires to get all the elements along.
At a turn, they begin to be,
A new parallel universe altogether.
Ahead of times,
Before the frills and wrinkles passed the test,
Of the sheathed model of absence,
A new fate grew into the present.
Change is season, of springs and winters,
A cyclic loop of existence,
Yet again, ahead in time,
Time sets the range.

Perks Of Pain

Pain is not normal,
It never is,
For it is a learning,
Of what normal looks like.

At normal times,
You can't be in praise of what normal is.
Only at not so normal times,
You are made to realize,
Of all the times which are rather normal,
Than better assumed to be so.

Normalcy is a gift,
Not often appreciated for being so.
Until unless there comes a time,
So different than what normal is.

Perks of pain,
Is a sure gain.
One's to make peace,
With the upcoming change.

On a deep vertical of thought,
Pains are perhaps like sediments,
But they make you aware,
Of the clearer water you are in at present.

Master Plans Of Amateur

Always a beginner,
As a learner,
To define the unlimited knowledge,
To gain in an everlasting loop.

A master is born,
Of the continued art of learned,
Yet like a practitioner,
Practices it like a breath of being.

Making a difference,
Like a teacher,
Candle by heart,
Pulley by function,
It is an art to be one.

Being amateur is the start,
The will to be better is the fulcrum,
When the tension and the time is right,
One is a control by themselves.

Toss Of A Coin

Flip side of two stories
About the same reality
Yet, seems so assorted,
When heard out of two different sources.

A replica, seems so alike,
Yet could be said apart from original.
Likewise, a tendency,
To ignore the granted,
To assume what is given,
That it shall stay forever,
Unknown of the very fact
That nothing lasts forever,
A ceiling to false assurance, that still remains.

Toss of a coin,
Where you are this close to deciding,
Of which side you are on,
While ignoring the very equal chance
of the occurrence of the other.
All remains sealed,
If you let that toss remain in the air,
And not expect anything of the two.

Wilted Boundaries

Bound by conflicts,
boundaries and not borders,
Fought by strands of grouped fences,
Grounded they stay like soil.

Rooted and deep drilled into the ground,
Like some guarded secrets,
Which can't be let out in open,
To dictate the terms out routines are to be led.

Restore, as we begin again,
To retain some and detain the rest,
Like those breakthrough patterns,
To put rest to decay and be born to nourish.

Bold Choices

Renunciation, it is a start,
To own up to the origin,
To speed up to the end state,
To fill the circle of life.

It isn't just a bold choice,
It is a designed path
That you are destined to take,
To enter the holy globe.

The entirety and eternity,
Are parts of the same loop,
Within one another.
A bold thread,
A choice of divine,
To live through the symbols of coexistence.

If you were to assume,
A choice that is of your own,
The gift of thought,
Is too a magic of nature,
That you still fail to accept,

Only to accept late,
It was all a play,
To bring things in place,
To where they belong.

Off The Cliff

While you push someone off the cliff,
remember that they climb again.
Be sure whether or not they avenge,
you are a scar that still remains.

With them, in their memories,
You stay as a nightmare,
For you leave them to dream,
Against all the good dreams they could ever
have.

It's not the height, but the depth,
That matters of how gravely it hurts,
Of nullifying the trust that someone
Had placed on you with full faith.

Time shall then soon come,
If you regret the same or not,
When the same happens to you,
With someone you trusted too deeply.

Obtain you shall then,
An understanding,
Of what it feels like,
To be pushed off the cliff,
while you once did the same in the past.

Thank You

Dear Poetry Lovers,

Thank you!

I know you understand how one feels and engages in poetry. Poetry is not just a form of expression; it is a whole language in itself. As though, each of the lines in the verses have something very intense and delicate to convey.

I appreciate you taking your time for my poetry. I truly hope you enjoyed these Coherent Conversations.

You can reach me on:
Twitter | Instagram - @piece_of_irony

I would love to hear your thoughts on how you connect with poetry and I am looking forward for many more connections to come along the way for it is just the beginning in this remarkable poetic world!

Who are We?

Dreams are limitless and so is our vision. Being **India's 1st "Lead by Authors" Publication House**, Lapsus Creations connect your dreams with vision.

With our **Guided Publishing approach**, authors will have their own dedicated team of experts working alongside for their **BOOK** to come alive. We guide them from the very initial stage of their writing journey till, and after the book is successfully published. While keeping quality at the forefront, we understand the needs of a writer and work towards fulfilling them **at zero extra cost.**

Promoting creativity across the world is what we are determined about. While we work on the dreams of our authors, we alongside take care of their choices too.

With Lapsus Creations authors have the leverage to choose what they want for their dream book.

We firmly believe in - Of the Authors, By the Authors, For the Authors.

Every dream has the right to get connected to its vision and Lapsus Creations has taken this initiative. Publishing every dream is our vision and hence we thrive on our motto

DREAM! VISION! LET'S CONNECT?

www.ingramcontent.com/pod-product-compliance
Lightning Source LLC
LaVergne TN
LVHW010609160826
845677LV00013B/3328

* 9 7 8 8 1 9 4 2 1 1 2 3 5 *